CRACK
YOURSELF
≈UP≈
JOKES FOR KIDS

Books by Author

The Great Bible Adventure

The All-Time Awesome Bible Search

In Search of Righteous Radicals

The Awesome Book of Bible Facts

Boris Is Missing!

Marpel Is Stuck!

Sarah Is Scared!

Gregory Is Grouchy

ReaLife Devotional Bible

Surviving Middle School

Surviving When You're Home Alone

Surviving Zits

One-Minute Mysteries and Brain Teasers

Return of the One-Minute Mysteries and Brain Teasers

Mind-Boggling One-Minute Mysteries

101 Awesome Bible Facts for Kids

Wild and Wacky Bible Stories for Kids

The Awesome Book of Unusual Bible Heroes for Kids

Amazing Tips to Make You Smarter

Two Truths and a Tall Tale

The Awesome Book of Bible Comics

CRACK YOURSELF UP

JOKES FOR KIDS

SANDY SILVERTHORNE

SPIRE

© 2018 by Sandy Silverthorne

Published by Revell
a division of Baker Publishing Group
PO Box 6287, Grand Rapids, MI 49516-6287
www.revellbooks.com

ISBN 978-0-8007-2969-1

Printed in the United States of America

Author is represented by WordServe Literary Group (www.wordserveliterary.com)

18   19   20   21   22   23   24   7   6   5   4   3   2   1

To Vicki and Christy—
You guys are such a huge gift to me.
You always make me smile. Thanks for
not minding when I crack myself up.

And to the kids whom I have the privilege
to speak to every year—you're the best!

Do you like to crack your friends up? Do you like to crack your parents up? How about your teachers? Your brothers and sisters? Most of all, do you like to crack *yourself* up? Then you came to the right place. This fun, crazy joke book is filled with the greatest jokes, stories, knock knocks, and riddles in the world.

It's also got some really nutty cartoons to go along with them. So get to it. Get ready to read. Get ready to chuckle. And get ready to crack yourself up!

Q: What musical instrument is found in the bathroom?

A: A tuba toothpaste.

Q: What's red and smells like blue paint?

A: Red paint.

Q: What kind of lights did Noah use on the ark?

A: Flood lights.

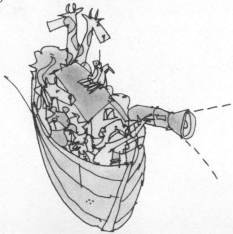

Q: Where do pencils go on vacation?

A: Pencilvania.

Q: What did the janitor say when he jumped out of the closet?

A: SUPPLIES!

SUPPLIES!

Q: What did the ocean say to the shore?

A: Nothing; it just waved.

Q: What do porcupines say when they kiss?

A: Ouch.

If Ella from *Ella Enchanted* married Darth Vader would she be Ella Vader?

Mason: How can you make sure you never wake up sleepy and grumpy?

Jason: Don't have a sleepover with the Seven Dwarfs.

Bill: My grades are underwater.
Phil: What do you mean?
Bill: They're below C level.

Terry: When they built the Great Wall of China
where did the workers go for supplies?
Jerry: Wal-Mart of course.

If Cardinal Sicola were to become the pope, would he be Pope Sicola?

Q: What did the hamburger name his daughter?

A: Patty.

Jim: Why do birds fly south for the winter?
Tim: It's so much faster than walking.

Q: What do Alexander the Great and Winnie the Pooh have in common?

A: Same middle name.

Q: What do you call a pile of kittens?

A: A meowtain.

Q: What's red and goes up and down?

A: A tomato in an elevator.

Did you hear about the corduroy pillows?
They're making headlines.

Little Girl: Mommy, you've got some gray hairs.

Mom: Yes, every time you don't behave, I get another gray hair.

Little Girl: Is that why Grandma has so many?

Ron: Come see this photo of my aunt.

Don: That's a picture of a fish!

Ron: I know. It's my anchovy!

Teacher: Samuel, use the word *boycott* in a sentence.

Samuel: The boycott four fish and his sister only caught three.

Teacher: Sophie, use the word *information* in a sentence.

Sophie: Ducks fly information when they're heading south.

A guy walks into a lawyer's office and asks what he charges.

"I charge $1,000 for three questions," the lawyer answered.

"Wow, that's pretty expensive isn't it?" the man said.

"Yes it is," said the lawyer. "What's your third question?"

I couldn't believe it when the Highway Department called my dad a thief. But when I got home all the signs were there.

Knock, knock.

Who's there?

Lettuce.

Lettuce who?

Lettuce in! We're freezing out here!

Knock, knock.

Who's there?

Pizza.

Pizza who?

Pizza really great guy, don't you think?

Knock, knock.
Who's there?
Dishes.
Dishes who?
Dishes your father speaking. Open the door!

Man:	Doctor, you've got to help me. I'm convinced I'm a cocker spaniel.
Psychiatrist:	Come in and lie down on the couch.
Man:	I can't. I'm not allowed on the furniture!

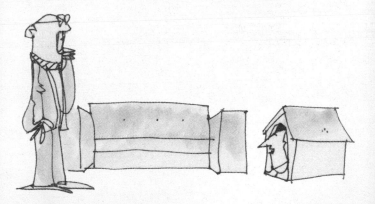

Q: Why did the skeleton stay home from the dance?

A: Because he had no-body to go with him.

Q: What music scares balloons?

A: Pop music.

Donny: So what are you doing today?
Lonny: Nothing.
Donny: Nothing? That's what you did all day yesterday.
Lonny: I know. I'm not finished yet.

Q: Why is England so wet?

A: Because the Queen has reigned there for years.

Q: Why did the lawyer bring a briefcase and a ladder to the courtroom?

A: He wanted to take his case to a higher court.

Braeden: I just got two cupcakes for my brother.
Caden: Wow, that was a good swap.

My doctor told me to play 18 holes every day.
So I took up the harmonica.

Len: I fell off a thirty-foot ladder yesterday.
Ben: Wow! Are you okay?
Len: Yeah, I was only on the second rung.

Did you hear about the missing barber?
    Police are combing the city.

Knock, knock.

Who's there?

Radio.

Radio who?

Radio not, here I come!

Knock, knock.

Who's there?

Old Lady.

Old Lady who?

Wow, you can yodel!

Q: What kind of cars do kittens drive?

A: Catillacs.

Q: What did the judge say when the skunk walked in the courtroom?

A: Odor in the court.

Q: What goes "Tick Tick Woof Woof"?

A: A Watchdog.

Ed: Why did the soft drink can presser quit his job?

Ned: Because it was soda pressing.

Q: What has three letters and starts with gas?

A: A car.

      Patient: Doctor, I feel like a butterfly.
Psychiatrist: Have you always felt this way?
      Patient: No, a couple years ago I felt like a caterpillar.

Q: What do a dog and a telephone have in common?

A: Both have a collar ID.

Q: What do you call a dinosaur with a good vocabulary?

A: A Thesaurus.

Q: Why do seagulls fly over the sea?

A: Because if they flew over the bay they'd be called bagels!

Q: What did the lawyer name his daughter?

A: Sue.

Your light isn't working. You need to get off your bike.

I tried that, but the light still doesn't work.

Q: What do you get when you cross a rooster with a giraffe?

A: An animal who wakes people who live on the top floor.

Q: Why are dogs such bad dancers?

A: They have two left feet.

Diner: Waiter, do you have frog legs?
Waiter: Yes.
Diner: Then hop over here and take my order.

Diner: Waiter, what's this fly doing in my soup?
Waiter: It appears to be the backstroke.

Diner: Waiter, this soup is awful. Who made it?
Waiter: We all had a hand in it.

Joe: I went for seven days without sleep and I'm not even tired.
Flo: Wow! How did you do it?
Joe: I slept at night.

Diner: Waiter, how long have you worked here?
Waiter: Three months.
Diner: Oh, then you weren't the one who took my order.

Diner: Waiter, get your thumb off my waffles!
Waiter: And have them fall on the floor again?

Sir, the invisible man is
    out in the reception room.

Tell him I can't see him.

Gladys: I keep seeing spots before my eyes.
Mabel: Have you seen a doctor?
Gladys: No, just these spots.

Boss: You made a fool out of me!
Worker: I can't take all the credit. You do a pretty good job yourself.

A little boy went with his grandmother to his first ballet.

After watching the dancers on their toes for most of the performance, he turned to Grandma and said, "If they'd wanted taller dancers why didn't they just hire some?"

Q: Why did Tyler tiptoe past the medicine cabinet?

A: He didn't want to wake the sleeping pills!

Man: Doctor, every time I drink a cup of coffee, I get a sharp pain in my eye.
Doctor: Try taking the spoon out before you drink it.

Diner: I refuse to eat this steak! Call the manager.
Waiter: It's no use. He won't eat it either.

Waiter: And how did you find your steak, sir?
Diner: Easy—I just moved the mashed potatoes and there it was!

A soccer player was yelling at his own goalie, "Why didn't you stop the ball?"

The goalie replied, "Excuse me. I thought that's what the net was for!"

Duchess: Will you join me in a cup of tea?
   Duke: Do you think we can both fit?

Turkey Mom to her chick: You're behaving so badly, your father must be rolling over in his gravy!

Movie Theater Ticket Seller: Sir, that's the sixth ticket you've bought.
Moviegoer: I know. That guy by the rope keeps tearing them up.

Q: A box is filled with water and weighs 1,000 pounds. What can you add to it to make it lighter?

A: Holes.

Phil: My wife and I are going to the Caribbean.
Will: Jamaica?
Phil: No, she wanted to go.

Teacher: What did George Washington say after he crossed the Delaware River?
Jack: Everybody out of the boat!

Are we there yet?

Q: What happens to a frog who overparks?

A: He gets toad.

Ben: What's the difference between an elephant and a mailbox?

Len: I don't know.

Ben: Well, I'm not sending you to mail a letter.

Bill: Will you remember me in a day, a week, a month?

Jill: Absolutely. I'll never forget you.

Bill: Knock, knock.

Jill: Who's there?

Bill: You said you'd remember me!

Q: How does a mermaid call her friends?

A: On her shell phone.

Q: What do you call a polar bear wearing earmuffs?

A: Anything you want. He can't hear you!

Hello? Can you hear me now?

Q: What's brown and sticky?

A: A stick.

Q: What do you call a belt made out of watches?

A: A waist of time.

Q: How do you count cows?

A: With a cowculator.

Q: What kind of shoes do frogs wear?

A: Open toad.

Peg: What is green and brown and crawls
through the grass?

Meg: A Girl Scout who lost her cookie.

A man was talking to God one day.

"Lord, is it true that to you a million years is like a minute?"

"Yes, that's true."

"And a million dollars is like a penny?"

"Yes, that's true too."

The man hesitated. "Lord, will you give me a penny?"

"In a minute."

A little girl was drawing a picture in her Sunday school class.

The teacher asked, "What are you drawing, Natalie?"

"I'm drawing a picture of God," she answered.

"But nobody knows what God looks like," the teacher said.

Natalie smiled and said, "They will in a minute."

Mom: Why are you scratching yourself, Alfie?
Alfie: 'Cause no one else knows where I itch.

Mick: Did you know that deep breathing kills germs?
Dick: Yes, but how do I get them to breathe deeply?

Customer: Will the band play anything I ask them to?
Bandleader: Sure.
Customer: Then ask them to play chess.

Boss: What were you before you started working here?
Jamie: Happy.

Nate: My teacher was mad because I didn't know where the pyramids were.

Mom: Well, try to remember where you put things.

Salesman: This computer will do half your work for you.

Customer: In that case, I'll take two.

Customer: I think I can put this wallpaper on myself.
Salesman: Go ahead, but most people prefer to put it on the wall.

Susie was so excited that she put together a puzzle in just 10 days even though the box said 2–4 years.

Q: What do you get when you cross a stream and a brook?

A: Wet feet.

Teacher: "Whoever answers my next question can go home."

A boy throws his backpack out the window.

"Who threw that?" the teacher said.

"I did," the boy answered. "I'm going home."

A blonde yells to another blonde across the river, "How do I get to the other side?"

"You *are* on the other side!"

In a school cafeteria there was a small sign that said, "Please take just one apple. God is watching."

At the end of the counter by the tray of cookies, someone had scribbled out another sign that said, "Take all the cookies you want. God is watching the apples."

Principal: Where were you born, son?

Tyler: In the United States.

Principal: Which part?

Tyler: All of me.

Kid: My dad's a magician. He saws people in half.
Syd: Wow. Do you have any siblings?
Kid: Three half sisters and a half brother.

Q: Why was Cinderella thrown off the basketball team?

A: 'Cause she ran away from the ball.

Q: Why did the baby cookie cry?

A: Because his father was a wafer so long.

Q: What do ducks watch on TV?

A: Duckumentaries

Teacher: In the Bible, Lot was told to take his wife and flee out of the city. His wife looked back and turned to salt.

Student: What happened to the flea?

Bill: Did you hear that Marvin got a job as a ditch digger?

Phil: Great. How did that happen?

Bill: He just fell into it.

Q: What do you call a guy lying on your doorstep?

A: Matt.

Knock, knock.

Who's there?

Stopwatch.

Stopwatch who?

Stopwatch you're doing and open the door!

Q: How do you keep a rhino from charging?

A: Take away his credit card.

Q: What washes up on tiny beaches?

A: Microwaves.

Q: When is it bad luck to have a black cat following you?

A: When you're a mouse.

Q: What do you call it when dinosaurs crash their cars?

A: Tyrannosaurus Wrecks.

Kyle stole the ketchup, but the cops caught him red-handed.

Q: Where do vegetables volunteer?

A: The Peas Corps.

Q: What is heavy forward but not backward?

A: Ton.

Apparently I snore so loudly it scares all the people in the car I'm driving.

Whenever I fill out an application, in the line that says who to contact in case of an emergency, I always write down "doctor."

Dolphins are so smart they teach people to stand by the pool and toss them fish.

Don: Why did the kid put a flashlight in his suit
of armor?

Ron: He wanted to make a Knight-Light.

Rowan: Hey Ava, what do you say to a nice walk?

Ava: That sounds lovely.

Rowan: Good, will you pick me up some donuts
and chips while you're out there?

Mack: According to statistics, a person is robbed
in Chicago every seven minutes.

Mike: That poor guy should consider moving.

Tried to catch fog yesterday. Mist.

Q: What does a pirate who just turned 80 say?

A: Aye Matey!

Knock, knock.

Who's there?

Gorilla.

Gorilla who?

Gorilla me up a hamburger.

Knock, knock.

Who's there?

Amish.

Amish who?

Sweet, I miss you too.

Knock, knock.

Who's there?

Alex.

Alex who?

Alex the questions around here.

Q: What did the elevator say to the other elevator?

A: I think I'm coming down with something.

Did you hear about the two guys who stole a calendar?

They each got six months.

My favorite nation in the world? Donation! Give me 10 bucks.

Q: What do you call birds who stick together?

A: Velcrows.

Q: What's gray and can't fly?

A: A parking lot.

Coworker: Excuse me, can I disturb you for a second?

Walt: Sure, what is it?

Coworker: Nothing. I just wanted to disturb you.

Chad: It's times like this I wish I'd listened to what my dad always said.

Rad: What did he say?

Chad: I don't know. I wasn't listening.

Q: What's white and sits on your TV?

A: A fly wearing a nightgown.

Q: What would happen if you threw blue tennies into the Red Sea?

A: They'd get wet.

Man: Please send the ambulance! My wife is having a baby!

Operator: Okay, calm down. Is this her first child?

Man: No, this is her husband!

Q: This guy shaves 15 times a day but still has a beard. How come?

A: He's a barber.

Diner: Waiter, I can't possibly eat all this. Could I have a doggy bag to take it home?

Waiter: Sir, this is the buffet table.

Officer: Your driver's license, please.

   Susie: So sorry, I forgot.

Officer: At home?

   Susie: No, to get one.

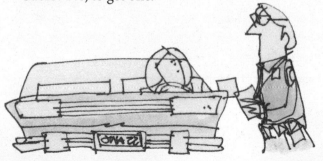

My teacher told me to have a good day, so I went home.

Did you hear about the guy who made a photocopy then compared it to the original to make sure there were no spelling errors?

Candy: Did you have any trouble with the test questions?

Andy: Not at all. It was the answers that were a pain.

The main reason for a child's middle name— so he can tell when he's really in trouble.

Is this letter for you?
The name's all blurry.

No, my name is Anderson.

Did you hear about the popcorn truck accident at the army base?

Three kernels were lost.

Max: Grandma, how old are you?
Grandma: 39 and holding.
Max: How old would you be if you let go?

Q: What did one plate say to the other one?
A: Dinner's on me!

Q: What sport do you play with a wombat?
A: Wom, of course.

Teacher: Sam, what two days of the week start with T?
Sam: Today and Tomorrow!

Q: What did the tie say to the hat?

A: You go on a head. I'll just hang around.

Q: Why is the math book so sad?

A: Because it's got so many problems.

Madame: Why didn't you water the plants yesterday?
Jeeves: It was raining, ma'am.
Madame: Don't make excuses. You could have used
an umbrella.

Q: What's green and sings?

A: Elvis Parsley.

I'd like to get a job cleaning mirrors.
It's really something I could see myself doing.

A guy discovered four penguins wandering around his backyard.

His neighbor peeked over the fence and said, "What have you got there?"

"Some penguins. I don't know where they came from."

"You should take them over to the zoo."

"Good idea." So he loaded them into the back of his pickup.

The next day the neighbor saw the man loading the penguins into his pickup truck again.

"I thought you were taking those birds to the zoo."

"I did. We had such a nice time that today we're going to Disney World."

Penguins are half price on Tuesdays.

Brian: My uncle is a big shot. He's got 3,000 people under him.

Ryan: Is he a CEO?

Brian: No, he cuts the grass in a cemetery.

Tad: What does a clock do when it's hungry?

Rad: It goes back four seconds.

A mom texts her son: What do IDK, LY, and TTYL mean?

Son: I Don't Know, Love You, and Talk to You Later.

Mom: Okay. I'll try asking someone else.

Q: If cakes are 66 cents each, how much are upside-down cakes?

A: 99 cents.

Q: What do you get if you cross an electric blanket with a toaster?

A: People who pop out of bed in the morning.

Health Inspector: I'm afraid you have too many roaches in here.
Restaurant Owner: How many am I allowed?

Q: Who isn't your brother or your sister but is still the child of your parents?

A: You.

Knock, knock.

Who's there?

Summons.

Summons who?

Summons at the door.

Upset Patient: Doctor, I'm convinced I'm a pair of curtains.

Psychiatrist: Well stop complaining and pull yourself together.

Were you long in the hospital?

No, I was about the same size as I've always been.

Jason is such a dummy that during a power failure at the mall, he got stuck on an escalator for two and a half hours.

Lyle: Why did Sam leave his job?
Kyle: Illness.
Lyle: Really?
Kyle: Yeah, his boss got sick of him.

Man: Doctor, I'm convinced I'm a deck of cards.
Doctor: Wait here. I'll deal with you in a minute.

Boss: Look at this office. It looks like it hasn't been cleaned in over a month!
Gus: Don't blame me! I've only been here since Thursday.

I've been taking French lessons because we're adopting a baby from France. That way I'll be able to understand what he says when he starts talking.

Gladys: I made the chicken soup.
Chauncey: Thank goodness. I thought it was for us.

Remy: When is a car not a car?
Rowan: When it turns into a driveway.

Isabel: When is a door not a door?
Charlotte: When it's ajar.

Ron: Is this bug spray good for mosquitoes?
Jon: No way. It'll kill them.

Sal: You'd be a good dancer if it wasn't for two things.
Hal: What are those?
Sal: Your feet.

I'm reading a book about antigravity.
I can't put it down.

Bob: I have a photographic
memory.
Rob: Too bad it never
developed.

Christy: I lost my contact lens.
Misty: Where did you lose it?
Christy: Over by the bookcase.
Misty: Then why are you looking
for it over here?
Christy: Because the light is so much better here.

There are only three kinds of people.
Those who can count, and those who can't.

Mom: Noah, why are you so upset?

Noah: I just got an invitation to a birthday party. It says 4–7 and I can't go 'cause I'm eight!

Singer: I take requests.

Diner: Good. Can you sing "Far, Far Away"?

Dad: How do you like school, Aiden?

Aiden: Closed.

Alex: Dad, would you do my math for me?
Dad: No, it wouldn't be right.
Alex: Oh, you don't understand it either?

Addie: My aunt's a kleptomaniac.
Abby: Is she taking anything for it?

Girl: I'm tan from the sun.
Boy: Hi, I'm Jacob from the Earth.

I've told you a million times—don't exaggerate!

Officer: How did you manage to crash your car?
Driver: See that telephone pole over there?
Officer: Yeah.
Driver: Well, I didn't.

A young man came in to speak to the father of the girl he was planning to marry.

"Son, before you can marry my daughter, tell me—can you support a family?" the dad asked.

"I can support us," the young man answered, "but you're on your own."

"The horse I bet on was a real champion," the Texan bragged. "It took seven others to beat him."

Movie Star: My fan letters keep three secretaries busy.
    Agent: Answering them?
Movie Star: No, writing them.

Q: What dog do you find at an embassy?
A: A Diplomutt.

Q: Why did the clock get kicked out of class?
A: It tocked too much.

Jim: What has 18 legs and goes crunch, crunch, crunch?

Tim: A baseball team eating potato chips.

Q: What do you get when you cross the Invisible Man with an elephant?

A: A big nothing.

Grandpa: The town I grew up in was really small.

Kid: How small was it?

Grandpa: Our zip code was a fraction.

Ryan: Why are you moving to another state?

Brian: I read that 90 percent of accidents happen within five miles of your home.

Shopper: Do you have any loafers?
Shoe Store Clerk: We certainly do.
Shopper: Well, have one of them come over here and wait on me.

Knock, knock.

Who's there?

Nod.

Nod who?

Nod you again.

Did you hear about the guy who swallowed a dictionary?

He didn't breathe a word of it to anyone.

Kid: Dad, will you buy me a drum set?
Dad: Are you kidding? There's way too much noise around here already.
Kid: That's okay! I'll only practice when you're asleep.

Teacher: Do you think you can sleep in my class?
Student: I could if you wouldn't talk so loud.

Teacher: The law of gravity explains why we stay on the ground.
Student: How did we do it before the law was passed?

Teacher: David, what's another name for a bunch
of bees?

David: A great report card!

Did you hear about the guy who kept a bicycle in
his bedroom?

He was tired of walking in his sleep.

Lady: Hello, Fire Department? My garage is on fire!

Fireman: Okay, stay calm. How do we get there?

Lady: Oh, I think you should drive your big, red fire truck.

Diner: I'd like the special and coffee with no cream.

New Waitress: I'm sorry, we're out of cream. Would you like it with no milk instead?

Teacher: Joey, if you had twenty dollars in your front pocket, thirty dollars in your back pocket, and fifty dollars in your side pocket, what would you have?

Joey: Someone else's pants!

Jon: Why are you wearing those loud socks?

Ron: 'Cause my feet keep falling asleep.

Kylie: Why are you putting lipstick on your forehead?

Chloe: I'm trying to make up my mind.

Q: What do they call the time in history when nerds ruled the land?

A: The Dork Ages.

Q: How do you make antifreeze?

A: Take away her blanket.

Knock, knock.

Who's there?

Althea.

Althea who?

Althea later, alligator.

Mrs. Bailey: My husband just got run over by a
steamroller! What should I do?

Doctor: Tell him to lie flat on his back.

Josh: Dad, I lost my pet snake.
Dad: You need to put up signs around the neighborhood.
Josh: That won't help—he can't read.

Mom: How was your first day of school, Danny?

Danny: Oh, not so good. The teacher said, "Danny, I want you to sit here for the present." So I did. All day. And I never got the present!

Teacher: Have you ever traced your ancestors?

Asher: No, I'm not that good at drawing.

Q: What did the contractor say to the electrician when he arrived to the work site at noon?

A: Wire you insulate?

Bo: Why did Jimmy hit his head on the piano keys?

Jo: He was learning to play by ear.

A man went into the hospital for some tests. As he lay on the table a big black Labrador came in the room and sniffed all around him. After he left, a cat came in and jumped up on the table and explored the guy from head to toe. When the man got home he got a bill for $1,500.

"What was this for?" he exclaimed as he called the hospital.

"Oh," she said as she looked at the man's records, "that was for the Lab Test and the Cat Scan."

Q: How do grizzlies like to walk on the beach?

A: Bearfoot.

My parents always had to pay my brother to be good.
But not me—I was good for nothing!

Q: What's an alien's favorite snack?

A: Martian-mellows.

Q: What kind of music do planets listen to?

A: Neptunes.

Q: What kind of horses go out after dark?

A: Nightmares.

Q: What's a light-year?

A: A regular year but with fewer calories.

Rowan: Why did Rose go out with her purse wide open?

Remy: She heard there was going to be some change in the weather.

Q: Who's in charge of the pencil box?

A: The ruler!

Teacher: What happens when you touch a
window?

Smart Kid: You feel the pane.

Farmer Brown: What do cows use in their text
messages?

Mrs. Brown: E-moo-jis.

tap
tap
tap

Mike: Why did the chicken cross the road?

  Ike: To see the dumb guy.

Mike: Knock, knock.

  Ike: Who's there?

Mike: The chicken.

Doctor: There's good news and bad news. The good news is you're to take one of these pills a day for the rest of your life.

Patient: But there are only seven pills in here.

Doctor: That brings us to the bad news.

Q: What's black and white and eats like a horse?
A: A zebra.

Q: What is the Tower of Pisa's first name?
A: Eileen.

Knock, knock.
Who's there?
Mikey.
Mikey who?
Mikey doesn't work. Will you open the door?

Teacher: Timmy, what did you write your report on?
Timmy: A piece of paper.

Deagan: Why did the man put bandages in his refrigerator?

Hannah: He wanted some cold cuts.

Q: What kind of pig likes to drive a car?

A: A road hog.

Q: Why didn't the sun go to grad school?

A: 'Cause it already had a million degrees.

Q: What becomes shorter when you add two letters to it?

A: Short.

Q: What did the duck say when he bought lip balm?

A: Just put it on my bill.

Q: How do lumberjacks get onto the internet?

A: They log in.

Two brothers, Jamie and Sam, were deciding who got to eat the last waffle. Mom came in and suggested, "Boys, don't you think Jesus would want you to share? I think he would give his waffle to his brother."

"That's a good idea," Sam said. "Jamie, you be Jesus."

Math Teacher: If you have 10 apples in one hand and 13 oranges in your other hand, what do you have?

Thomas: Big hands!

Teacher: James, where was the Constitution of the United States signed?

James: At the bottom!

Where do we sign this thing?

Aiden: Why did Grandma put roller skates on her rocking chair?

Caden: 'Cause she wanted to rock and roll.

Knock, knock.

Who's there?

Samurai.

Samurai who?

Samurai will pick you up after school.

Knock, knock.

Who's there?

Butter.

Butter who?

Butter come over here and answer the door!

Q: Why is a river so rich?

A: Because it has two banks.

Q: Where does a track and field athlete keep his money?

A: In the pole vault.

Q: Where do pigs go on sunny Saturdays?

A: Pignics.

Max: Can you help me? I'm looking for where I can get an ark.

Jax: Oh, I Noah guy.

On a huge sailing ship the galley master went below deck and addressed the men who were rowing in the hull.

Galley Master: I've got good news and bad news. The good news is there will be more food rations tonight!

Men: Hooray! What's the bad news?

Galley Master: The captain wants to go water skiing.

FASTER!

Q: What is a mummy's favorite kind of music?

A: Wrap music, of course.

Knock, knock.

Who's there?

Nunya.

Nunya who?

Nunya business.

Knock, knock.

Who's there?

Kent.

Kent who?

Kent you tell? I'm standing right here!

Q: Where do cows go on a date?
A: To the moo-vies.

Knock, knock.
Who's there?
Harry.
Harry who?
Harry up and open the door!

Knock, knock.
Who's there?
Justin.
Justin who?
Justin time to tell you another knock knock joke.

Mr. Anderson: Were any famous men or women born on your birthday?

Joey: No, only little babies.

Patient: Doctor, you've got to help me. I think I'm losing my memory. I can't remember anything!

Doctor: How long have you had this problem?

Patient: What problem?

Q: Why did the baby join the army?

A: He wanted to be in the *infant*ry.

Q: What does the razor put in his coffee?

A: Shaving cream.

Teacher: James, how do you spell *crocodile*?
  James: K-R-O-C-I-D-I-L-E.
Teacher: That's wrong.
  James: Maybe, but you asked me how *I* spell it.

Teacher: Sammie, name one great thing that we have
         today that we didn't have 10 years ago.
Sammie: Me!

Policeman: I'm sorry, but your truck is way too overloaded. I'm going to need to take your license.

Truck Driver: Oh that won't help. It can't weigh more than two or three ounces.

Q: What's an ant's favorite country?

A: Frants.

Aiden was playing ball in his aunt's house when he missed and broke the vase that was on the mantle.

"Do you realize that vase was from the seventeenth century?" his aunt said. "It was over 300 years old!"

"Oh whew," Aiden said, "I was afraid it was new."

Q: What did one candle say to the other?

A: I'm going out tonight.

Q: What do you call a sleeping bull?

A: A bulldozer.

BACKWARD JOKES

Backward jokes give the answer first, then the question. Here's an example:

The answer is Kitty Litter.

The question is: "What does Garfield throw out the car window?"

Answer: Cyclone.

Question: What do you call a clone of a guy named Cy?

Answer: Supervisor.

Question: What does Superman wear to keep the sun out of his eyes?

Answer: Rose Bowl.

Question: What do you say when it's Rose's turn at the bowling alley?

Answer: Catch-22.

Question: What does a terrible baseball team do with 100 fly balls?

I GOT IT!!!

Answer: Mount Rushmore.

Question: What do you need to do to ride your horse named Rushmore?

Answer: Defense.

Question: What's between your and da neighbor's yard?

Answer: Despair.

Question: What are you glad you have in case of a flat tire?

Answer: Timbuktwo.

Question: What comes after Timbuc one?

Answer: Hoe Down.

Question: What does the farmer do when he's done working for the day?

Answer: Egg White.

Question: What is the name of Snow White's first child?

■ ■ ■ ■ ■

Knock, knock.

Who's there?

Wooden shoe.

Wooden shoe who?

Wooden shoe like to know.

Knock, knock.

Who's there?

Rita.

Rita who?

Rita book, and stop watching TV!

Q: How do astronauts keep in touch with each other?

A: Spacebook.

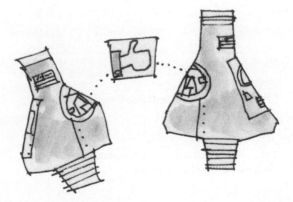

Q: What time do ducks get up?

A: At the quack of dawn.

Knock, knock.

Who's there?

Jenny.

Jenny who?

Jenny'd to open the door right now!

A blonde is scuba diving. Her friend is watching in admiration.

Friend: Why do you jump off the boat backward?

Blonde: If I jumped forward, I'd still be in the boat.

Why did you ask me to work out with you?

My doctor told me to exercise with dumbbells.

I went to a massage therapist, but I've stopped going. They rubbed me the wrong way.

Q: Where do young tigers swim?

A: In the kitty pool.

Q: What do you get when you cross cocoa with a herd of cows?

A: Chocolate Moos.

Q: What can you hold without touching it?

A: A conversation.

Q: What does a bee use to cut wood?

A: A buzz saw.

Q: What's a polar bear's favorite game?

A: Freeze tag.

Q: Why did the secret agent keep saying "1, 2, 3, 4, 5, 6, 7"?

A: He was a counterspy.

Q: What does a firefly order in a restaurant?

A: A light meal.

Alsea: Why do you have that lampshade on your head?

Max: I was feeling lightheaded.

Q: Why did the policeman open a bakery?

A: He wanted to make Copcakes.

Q: What has four wheels and honks?

A: A goose on a skateboard.

Q: What does a dog take on a camping trip?

A: A pup tent.

Q: Who invented the telephone and carries your luggage?

A: Alexander Graham Bellhop.

She loved the pastry chef, but always feared he'd dessert her.

It was Daddy's turn to read bedtime stories to his four-year-old son.

After about 20 minutes, Mom called up the stairs:

"Is he asleep?"

The little boy answered, "Yes, finally."

Randy: What's black and white and red all over?

Andy: A panda eating chili without utensils.

Jason: What do you get when you cross an honor
        student with a giraffe?
Mason: A kid everyone can look up to.

    Pat: Why can't you ever borrow money from a
          leprechaun?
Matt: 'Cause they're always a little short.

Q: When is a running boy not a boy?

A: When he's ahead in the race.

Logan: Ever see an egg roll?
Rogan: No, but I've seen an apple turnover.

Teacher: Conner, use the word *contrive* in a
sentence.
Conner: When I get my license I contrive.

Knock, knock.

Who's there?

Avenue.

Avenue who?

Avenue knocked on this door before?

Bo: I just read the weather forecast for Baja, California.

Jo: What is it?

Bo: Chili today and hot tamale.

Q: What's gray, has 400 feet, and never leaves the ground?

A: A plane full of elephants.

Q: What do you call a fly with no wings?

A: A walk.

Q: What bug is on the ground but also a hundred feet in the air?

A: A centipede on his back.

Q: When should you buy a bird?

A: When it's going cheep.

Q: What steals your stuff while you're in the bathtub?

A: A robber ducky.

Iris: Why did the spotted owl go to school?
Dad: I don't know. Why?
Iris: He wanted to study owlgebra.

Mom (on the first day of school): What did you learn today, Andy?
Andy: Not enough, apparently—they want me to come back tomorrow.

Teacher: Does anyone know who broke the sound barrier?
Manny: Don't ask me. I'm no tattletale.

Q: Why did the student bring his artist pad to the political speech?
A: He wanted to draw his own conclusions.

Q: Where do bunnies get their eyes checked?

A: At the Hoptometrist.

Q: What has a foot on each end and a foot in the middle?

A: A yardstick.

Teacher: Lucas, when I was your age I could do any math problem given to me.

Lucas: Yes, but you had a different teacher.

A dad and his son were out driving.

Dad: Oh no! I just went through that stop sign.

Son: Don't worry. The police car behind us did the same thing.

Robert: Do you want me to cut the pie into six pieces?

Grandma: Oh no. I could never eat six. Cut it into four.

Jan: My alarm clock went off at six this morning.

Dan: Did it ever come back?

Q: Did you hear about the acrobat who fell in love?

A: He was head over heels.

Don: I'm reading some books on plants.
Ron: Botany?
Don: No, I got them from the library.

Jo: Is it true you always answer one question with another?

Bo: Who told you that?

Jackson: Did you hear about the guy who ate 300 pancakes?

Jaden: How waffle!

Teacher: Jack, name two pronouns.

Jack: Who, me?

Teacher: Correct.

Q: Why did the millionaire never take a bath?

A: He wanted to be filthy rich.

I've been asking people what time it is since this morning, and everybody I ask tells me something different!

Mikey: Can you write in the dark, Dad?
Dad: I guess. What do you want me to write?
Mikey: Your name on this report card.

Peg: I can watch the sun rise from my bedroom.
Meg: So what? From my family room, I can watch the kitchen sink.

Bill: I used to wake myself up snoring.
Phil: What did you do to fix it?
Bill: Now I sleep in the other room.

Teacher: Stop acting like a fool!
Student: Who's acting?

Todd: My great-great-grandfather fought with Napoleon, my grandfather fought with the British, and my father fought with the Americans.

Tad: Boy, your family can't get along with anybody.

OH YEAH?

Logan: Your problem is you're always wishing for something you don't have.

Rogan: Well, what else is there to wish for?

Diner: Waiter, this coffee tastes like mud.

Waiter: Well, it was ground this morning.

Teacher: If you have five dollars and ask your father for five more, how much money would you have?

Sam: Five dollars.

Teacher: Boy, you don't know your math.

Sam: You don't know my father.

Hal: I'm back, and I've changed my mind.

Sal: Good. Does it work any better now?

Boss: What? Do you think I'm a perfect dummy?

Worker: Nonsense. Nobody's perfect.

Denny: What's the best way to prevent diseases caused by biting insects?

Penny: Don't bite any.

Phil: I swallowed a clock last week.

Doctor: Why didn't you tell me sooner?

Phil: I didn't want to alarm anybody.

Toby: Teacher, would you punish me for something I didn't do?

Teacher: No, of course not.

Toby: Good. I didn't do my homework.

Doctor: Have your eyes been checked lately?
  Caleb: No, they've always been solid brown.

 Mom: Did you take a bath today?
Lucas: Why? Is one missing?

 Mom: Eric, wake up! It's twenty to nine!
  Eric: In whose favor?

Josh is such a diligent student that last week he stayed up all night studying for a blood test.

Kid: Show me a tough kid, and I'll show you a big coward.

Bully: I'm a tough kid!

Kid: Well, I'm a big coward.

Customer: Why is my pizza all squished?

Pizza Guy: You said you wanted it that way.

Customer: I did?

Pizza Guy: Yeah, you said to give you a pizza and step on it!

Knock, knock.

Who's there?

Juicy.

Juicy who?

Juicy that shooting star?

Q: Where do cats go on vacation?

A: Meowmi Beach.

Q: Where do skunks sit in church?

A: In the pews.

Patient: Doctor, I still feel like I'm a worm. I'm not going to pay your bill.

Doctor: Oh yeah? You're not going to wiggle out of this one.

Q: What flies around the school at night?

A: An Alphabat.

Math Teacher: Jimmy, if you worked nine hours a day for a dollar an hour, what would you get?

Jimmy: A new job.

She loved her earthquake scientist despite his faults.

You really rock my world!

Chloe: What kind of shirts do army artillerymen wear?

Kylie: Tank tops!

Lon: What do wolves gargle with?

Don: Wolverine!

Salesman: This refrigerator will pay for itself in no time.

Customer: Good, send it over when it does.

This guy is so silly, he got water skis for his birthday. Now he's looking for a lake with a hill in it.

Johnny: Mom, may I join the track team?

Mom: Run that by me again.

Max: When I was a child my babysitter dropped me a lot.

Jax: What did your mom do?

Max: She got me a shorter babysitter.

Leon: Bob, have you seen Harvey?

Bob: Yeah, he's round in front.

Leon: I know what he looks like. I'm asking where he is.

Man: Hello, how much for a room?
Hotel Clerk: $150 a night.
Man: Do you take children?
Hotel Clerk: No, just cash or credit cards.

Mrs. Inverness: Do you have any great-grandchildren?
Mrs. Iverson: No, they're all pretty average.

Ron: My grandma fell down the stairs.
Jon: Cellar?
Ron: No, I think she can be repaired.

District Attorney: The court can produce dozens of witnesses who saw you rob that bank.
Criminal: So what? I can produce hundreds who didn't see me do it.

Customer: Buddy, will my pizza be long?
Pizza Guy: No, it'll be round just like all the others.

I've been reading article after article about how eating junk food is bad for you, so I made a New Year's resolution. From now on, no reading!

I'm so broke I can't even pay attention!

Growing up, our house was so small the mice were all hunchbacked.

Our house was so small that if you put the key in the front door, you broke the back window!

Q: What did William Shakespeare use when he got a flat?

A: His Shake-spare tire.

Q: What do you call an optometrist in the Aleutian islands?

A: An Optical Aleutian.

The teacher pointed at me with a ruler and said, "At the end of this ruler is a real dunce!"

I got sent to the principal's office when I said, "Which end?"

Q: What did the baseball glove say to the baseball?

A: Catch you later!

Q: Where do TVs go on vacation?

A: To remote places.

Customer: Have you got any kittens going cheap?
Pet Store Owner: No ma'am, all our kittens go meow.

Emily Biddle's Library of Book Titles:

Librarian Emily Biddle has a collection of unusual books in her bookmobile. Check out some of these titles:

1. *Wiring Your House* by Alec Tricity
2. *The Sinking of the Titanic* by Mandy Lifeboats
3. *The History of Russia* by Warren Peace
4. *Not a Guitar!* by Amanda Lynn
5. *What Is Lunch?* by Amelia Eat
6. *The Unknown Rodent* by A. Nonnie Mouse
7. *I'm Fine* by Howard Yu
8. *Learn Sky Diving* by Hugh First
9. *Police Story* by Laura Norder
10. *How to Annoy People* by Ann Tagonize

More Emily Biddle Book Titles:

Here are a few more interesting book titles from Emily's bookmobile:

1. *Pick Up that Penny!* by Ben Dover
2. *Strong Breezes* by Gustav Wind
3. *Why Christy Walked to School* by Mr. Buss
4. *Taking a Quick Shower* by I. C. Coldwater
5. *Why Won't My Car Run?* by M. T. Tank
6. *Let Me In!* by Isadore There
7. *What's that in the Swamp?* by Allie Gator
8. *Introduction to Arithmetic* by Adam Upp
9. *The Empty House* by Annie Buddyhome
10. *Coming In First* by Adam Myway

Would you like me to put the milk in the bag?

No, it can stay in the carton.

Sandy Silverthorne has been writing and illustrating books since 1988 and currently has over 600,000 copies in print. His award-winning *Great Bible Adventure* children's series sold over 170,000 copies and has been distributed in eight languages worldwide. He's written and illustrated over thirty books and has worked with such diverse clients as Universal Studios Tour, Doubleday Publishers, Penguin, World Vision, the University of Oregon, the Charlotte Hornets, and the Academy of Television Arts and Sciences. His recent series *One-Minute Mysteries* has already sold over 160,000 copies. Sandy has worked as a cartoonist, author, illustrator, actor, pastor, speaker, and comedian. Apparently it's hard for him to focus.

Connect with him at sandysilverthornebooks.com